Love is Full of
Surprises

*To Beckie, who taught me
that cuddles make you grow*

Text copyright © Jenny Hyson 2000
Illustrations copyright © Francis Blake 2000

The author asserts the moral right
to be identified as the author of this work

**Published by
The Bible Reading Fellowship**
Peter's Way, Sandy Lane West
Oxford OX4 6HG
ISBN 1 84101 174 6

First published 2000
10 9 8 7 6 5 4 3 2 1 0

All rights reserved

Acknowledgments
Unless otherwise stated, scripture quotations are taken from the Good News
Bible published by The Bible Societies/HarperCollins Publishers Ltd, UK
© American Bible Society 1966, 1971, 1976, 1992, used with permission.

A catalogue record for this book is available from the British Library

Printed and bound in Great Britain by Omnia Books Limited, Glasgow

Love is Full of Surprises

Jenny Hyson

Contents

Introduction	6
Love is more than words	8
God loves us and knows all about us	14
God's story is a love story	21
A new way to love	28
Love that is full of surprises	38
The battle between love and hate	46
Peter discovers just how much God loves him	51
A love that never lets go	58

Introduction

Sometimes, when you love someone very, very much, you want to find a way to describe how great your feelings are. Sometimes, saying, 'I love you' isn't enough. Sometimes we can feel shy about saying, 'I love you', so we might want to think of another way of showing our love.

The Bible is a storybook in which time and time again we can hear God saying, 'Guess how much I love you'. If we look carefully, we can see that God uses more than words. He tells us in many different and sometimes surprising ways that he loves us!

Something to think about

How many different ways can you think of to show someone how much you love them? Write or draw one idea in each of the heart shapes.

Love is more than words

The first surprising way that God showed us he loved us was to make a beautiful world for us to live in. Let's look at what the Bible tells us the world was like before God stepped in.

> *In the beginning, when God created the universe, the earth was formless and desolate. The raging ocean that covered everything was engulfed in total darkness.*
>
> Genesis 1:1–2

Imagine nothing but darkness and water.

But God made the light shine into the darkness. He called the light 'day' and the darkness he called 'night'. God didn't stop at that. He filled the night sky with shining stars and in the daytime sky he placed the warming sun.

Even then, God didn't stop. Next he divided the world into water and dry land. The waters he filled with all kinds of fish, large and small. On the dry land, plants, flowers, trees and all kinds of tasty fruits and things to eat began to grow.

Then God made all kinds of living creatures, some with four legs and some with six, eight or even more! All of them were different. Some were large and some were small. Some ran and others crawled or flew in the air.

Stop for a moment and try to imagine God creating the world. I wonder if he made some animals look funny on purpose, just to make us laugh?

Think about the giraffe with its long neck, the elephant with its long nose and the octopus with its eight legs!

Something to think about

Which animals make you laugh? Can you draw them in the picture space?

We know that God didn't just make animals and fishes, plants and birds. He also made people like you and me. He made us to be special. He loved us most of all and wanted us to have the *best* of everything. The Bible tells us that God didn't want us to live on our own. He wanted us to live together and help one another.

This is what the Bible says:

> *Then the Lord God said, 'It is not good for the man to live alone. I will make a suitable companion to help him.'*
>
> Genesis 2:18

Most of all, God wanted us to be *his* friends! He didn't want us to hide from him. He wanted us to talk to him about everything we do.

> *That evening the man and the woman heard the Lord God walking in the garden, and they hid from him among the trees. But the Lord God called out to the man, 'Where are you?'*
>
> Genesis 3:8–9

When God had finally finished making the world, he stopped and rested.

> *God looked at everything he had made, and he was very pleased. By the seventh day God finished what he had been doing and stopped working. He blessed the seventh day and set it apart as a special day.*
>
> Genesis 1:31 and 2:2–3

Today God still wants us to keep a day of the week special. Many people keep Sunday special. They use it as a time to rest, to go to church and to think especially about God.

When God made the world, he didn't make it just to keep for himself. He showed us how much he loved us by giving the world to us. He wanted us to enjoy the world and he trusted us to look after it.

A prayer to say

Thank you, God, for our beautiful world,
The flowers and trees, the birds and fishes.
Thank you especially for ....
And thank you for making me ME!

Think what it is like to make or draw something really beautiful and then give it to someone. How does it make you feel?

Giving a present is one of the ways we can show our love to our families and friends. Sometimes it is something we've bought, but sometimes it is something we have made. How do you think you would feel if you gave a present to someone and they spoilt it or broke it?

Sadly, we don't always care for God's world as much as he wants us to. There are times when we don't even notice how beautiful God's world really is and we ignore God's gift to us. How do you think that makes God feel?

Something to think about

Think for a moment about God's beautiful world. You might like to go outside or look out of a window. What can you see that is part of God's creation? What can you hear? What can you smell?

On one half of the heart shape, write or draw the thing in creation that you most enjoy. It might be a flower or a beetle, an animal or a crashing wave, a beautiful sunset or a starry sky.

Now think about the ways we spoil our world, not just when we leave rubbish around but when we don't love and care for one another. When we fight and make wars, and when people are left hungry and homeless, we spoil God's creation.

Something to think about

On the second half of the heart shape, draw or write one of the things that you think makes God sad about the way we don't care for the world.

Sometimes we are so busy that we don't really notice just how beautiful God's world is, but if you look carefully all around you at the world God made, you might be surprised to hear it whisper:

'God's love is full of surprises!'

God loves us and knows all about us

At a fair or a theme park, you sometimes find a 'Hall of Mirrors'. The mirrors make you look really funny—tall and skinny or short and tubby. Sometimes they make you look as though you have a long head, and sometimes they make your legs look as though they go on for ever! This kind of mirror doesn't give a very good image of what you really look like at all.

Look in a normal mirror and see what happens. When you smile, your reflection smiles back at you. When you look sad, your reflection looks sad, too.

The Bible tells us that when God made us, he made us to be like his reflection.

> *'They will be like us and resemble us.'*
>
> Genesis 1:26

I wonder what God meant.

Something to think about

Draw your reflection in this mirror.

A mirror only reflects what we look like on the outside. But when God made us to be like him, he wasn't thinking about the colour of our eyes or the shape of our noses. He was thinking about what we are like on the inside. The way we love and care for one another is much more important to God than what we look like. God gave us imaginations and brains so that we could be creative in the same way that he is creative. There are people who paint beautiful pictures, or write lovely music. There are people who build amazing buildings, or invent all kinds of useful gadgets. There are doctors and nurses who look after us when we are unwell, and scientists who can find out all about our world and how it works.

Something to think about

What kind of things do you like to make or do?

Look at yourself in the mirror and try to think about what you look like to God on the inside bit of you.

In the first mirror shape, write or draw the things you like about yourself. Now, in the broken mirror shape, write or draw the things that you don't like about yourself. Don't be too hard on yourself—remember, God loves you just the way you are.

 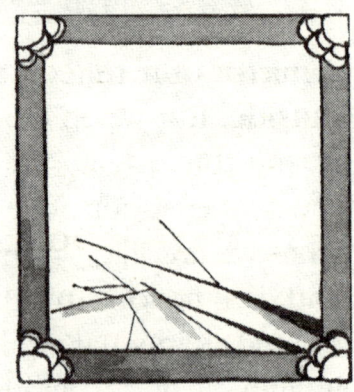

When we care about someone, we don't just bother about what they look like on the outside, but we try to discover more about who they really are. We find out what makes them laugh and what makes them cry, the things they like and the things that make them afraid. Did you know that God cares about you in just the same way?

The Bible tells us that God knows all about us—not in a way that is unkind and nosey, but in knowing who we really are and wanting what is best for us.

Look at these verses from Psalm 139 and see how God knew us even before we were born.

> *When my bones were being formed, carefully put together in my mother's womb, when I was growing there in secret, you knew that I was there.*
>
> Psalm 139:15

Isn't that an amazing thought?

Something to think about

Join the dots to make a picture of your skeleton. It is very clever, how it all works.

Psalm 139 also tells us that God knows everything we do. He also knows our thoughts and what we are going to say even before we say it.

Sometimes, when we do things wrong, we don't want others to know. Sometimes we hide so that we can't be seen. Sometimes we tell lies. But the psalm doesn't say that God is watching us to catch us out and tell us off when we do something wrong. It says something quite different. Have a look and see what it says.

> *You are all round me on every side; you protect me with your power.*
>
> Psalm 139:5

The writer of the psalm wondered if there was anywhere he could go where God couldn't find him, but he soon discovered the answer.

> *If I flew away beyond the east or lived in the farthest place in the west, you would be there to lead me, you would be there to help me.*
>
> Psalm 139:9–10

See how the writer of the psalm wasn't afraid of God watching over him all the time. He knew that God wanted to protect and care for him and he knew he could trust God to do just that.

Have a look in the mirror again and see if you can count how many hairs there are on your head. Impossible! When Jesus was explaining to his friends how much God knew them and cared for them, he told them this.

> *Even the hairs of your head have all been counted. So do not be afraid.*
>
> Luke 12:7

Why do you think Jesus told his friends this incredible fact? Maybe it was to help them to realize how important they were to God and just how much God loved them.

Sometimes it is hard to believe in someone we can't see. It's hard to understand how God can be with us all the time. But God's love and care can surprise us by coming to us through other people.

Remember how we are made in God's image? We are like a reflection of God. When we are being caring and helpful to others, we are reflecting God's love just like a mirror reflects the smile on your face. When other people are being kind and loving to us, they are being a reflection of God's love.

If you look carefully, you might see your reflection in a puddle. The reflection isn't always very clear. You can sometimes make out what the reflection is, but not as clearly as the real image.

Paul, who was one of the first people to tell others about Jesus, said that understanding God's love is a bit like this kind of blurred reflection. He wrote this:

> *What we see now is like a dim image in a mirror; then we shall see face to face.*
>
> 1 Corinthians 13:12

Something to think about

In the mirror shape, draw a reflection of someone who you think reflects God's love to you.

God's story is a love story

If you stand in the middle of a library or a large bookshop, you can look around at the shelves of books of all different kinds. They come in all shapes and sizes. Some have pictures and some are without pictures. Some books tell us about speaking another language. Some tell us things that happened hundreds of years ago. Then there are story books and picture books, poetry books and adventure books. Some books are true stories and some are imaginary.

Something to think about

I wonder which is your favourite type of book. In the book shape, draw or write the title of the book you've most enjoyed.

The Bible is like a library all in one book. It is made up of sixty-six books and they are all different. There are history stories, true-life stories and adventure stories. There are letters and poems, as well as instructions about how best to live. Some of the stories are biographies that tell of people's lives, while others are stories written as a way of explaining things to us about God and his love. Most of all, the Bible is a love story, and through its pages we can hear God saying over and over again:

'My love is full of surprises'

We've already found out that in the beginning, out of nothing but love, God created a beautiful world and gave it to us to care for. One of God's special friends was someone called Abraham. Abraham loved God and God showed his love for Abraham by promising him that he would have more children, grandchildren and great-grandchildren than there were stars in the sky. What a promise!

God promised Abraham that his descendants would be very special.

> *'I will make you my own people, and I will be your God.'*
>
> Exodus 6:7

The first part of the Bible is called the Old Testament. It is where we read about Abraham and his descendants. It is full of stories of how God loved and protected his special people just as he promised Abraham he would.

Look in the star shapes to see the names of some of the people who were Abraham's descendants. Do you recognize any of the names? Can you match the name with the story picture? Draw a line between the star and the picture.

Even though there were times when God's people turned away from him and did things that made him sad, God never gave up on them. Nothing they did could make him love them less.

> *'For one brief moment I left you; with deep love I will take you back. I turned away angry for only a moment, but I will show you my love for ever.'*
>
> Isaiah 54:7–8

Time and again, God tried to show his people how much he loved them and how much he wanted them to trust him. But time after time, they ignored God and tried to do things their own way. Special people, called prophets, who were very close to God, tried to tell the people how much God loved them, but still they wouldn't listen.

It was time for God to find a new way to show his love. When the time was right, God's son, Jesus, was born into the world. Jesus came to show everyone what God is like and how very much God loves us.

> *For God loved the world so much that he gave his only Son, so that everyone who believes in him may not die but have eternal life. For God did not send his Son into the world to be its judge, but to be its saviour.*
>
> John 3:16–17

It was time for God to write a new chapter in his book.

Cut out a strip of paper about 30 cm x 10 cm. Now fold the paper four times backwards and forwards to give five even spaces like a concertina. Write ABOUT ME at the top of the first space.

Something to think about

Now think about the following sentences and write or draw your answer, one in each of the folded spaces.

- The people who live with me
- Something which makes me happy
- Something which makes me sad
- My best friend
- Something funny that happened to me

Our lives are made up of lots of little stories. Sometimes those stories are happy and sometimes they are sad. We are also part of God's much bigger story.

God's story started with creation and is still going on today. His love and care are always in the world. In the Old Testament, written many thousands of years ago, we can see how God cared for his special people, the Israelites. In the New Testament, written just two thousand years ago, we can see how Jesus showed God's love to his friends. Ever since people have known about Jesus, all through the years, they have heard God say, 'Guess how much I love you'. And now God wants us to hear how much we are loved, too.

Something to think about

In the last space, write or draw something new you have learnt about God in this chapter.

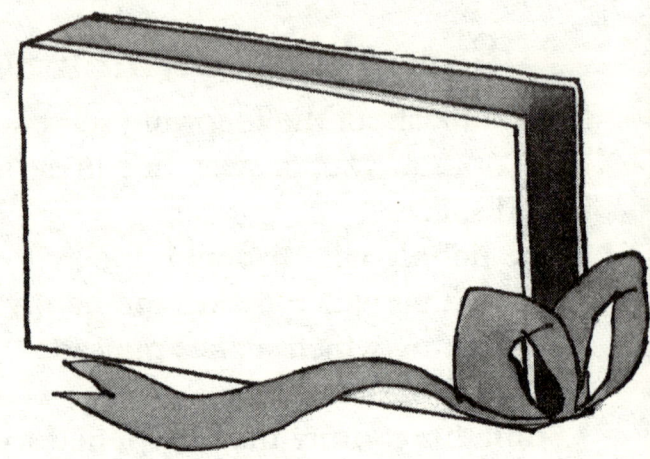

A prayer to say

Lord God, creator of all,
We thank you for the true story of your love.
Thank you for the story of our lives.
Thank you for the special story of Jesus' life.
And thank you that you want us to be part of your story of love.
Thank you that you never give up on us,
Even when we stop listening to you. Amen

A new way to love

The new chapter of how God showed his love for us began when Jesus was born, two thousand years ago. It may seem strange that God could show his love through a tiny baby but that was all part of how God would surprise us with a special plan.

Remember how the angel came to Mary and told her she was to have a special baby? The angel said that the baby would be God's son and Mary was to call him Jesus.

I expect, at first, Mary was frightened and confused by what the angel told her, but she already knew she could trust in God, and so she said:

> *'I am the Lord's servant; may it happen to me as you have said.'*
>
> Luke 1:38

Do you remember what happened next in the story?

Joseph went from the town of Nazareth in Galilee to the town of Bethlehem in Judea, the birthplace of King David. Joseph went there because he was a descendant of David. He went to register with Mary, who was promised in marriage to him. She was pregnant, and while they were in Bethlehem, the time came for her to have her baby. She gave birth to her first son, wrapped him in strips of cloth and laid him in a manger—there was no room for them to stay in the inn.

Luke 2:4–7

Did you notice the word 'descendant' again? Joseph was a descendant of David, and David was a descendant of Abraham!

A family tree is a way to find out what your aunts, uncles, grandparents and great-grandparents were called. If Jesus had drawn a family tree, he would have found that his earthly family was part of the Jewish nation—the people of Israel—who went all the way back to Abraham.

But Jesus grew up knowing that he also had a heavenly Father, who had sent him into the world with a special job to do. He was to tell the people about his Father God in heaven and how much he loved them.

Something to think about

How many names can you fill in on your family tree?

When Jesus was only eight days old, Mary and Joseph took him to the temple in Jerusalem to say 'thank you' to God for their new baby. It was the custom at that time to do this. It was also like trusting the new baby into God's care. While they were there, a wise old man named Simeon, who spent all his time in the temple worshipping God, came up to Mary and Joseph.

At once he saw that Jesus was no ordinary baby, but that he was the Messiah—God's special messenger—whom the prophets of long ago had spoken about.

Simeon gently took the baby Jesus into his arms. He had been praying for many years that he would not die before he saw the promised Messiah, and now here was this special baby, God's own son. He thanked God and then he spoke to Mary. He warned her that as Jesus grew up and began to talk about his heavenly Father, there would be those who would not like what he had to say.

> *'This child is chosen by God for the salvation of many in Israel. He will be a sign from God which many people will speak against.'*
>
> Luke 2:34

Poor Mary, I wonder what she thought as she heard Simeon's words.

Jesus grew up with Mary and Joseph in the town of Nazareth. Each Sabbath, the special day of rest, he would have gone with his family to the synagogue and listened to words read from the Jewish Bible, the Torah, which is the first five books of our own Bible. Jesus would have learnt about the customs and festivals of the Jewish faith as well as the Ten Commandments.

When Jesus was about thirty years old, he began to travel about, speaking to people about God. He showed people that there was a new way of loving one another.

One day, when Jesus was in the synagogue in Nazareth, he was handed the Jewish scriptures to read out loud. This would have been like reading the Old Testament lesson in church today, only Jesus wouldn't have read from a book but a long scroll of parchment paper.

Jesus unrolled the scroll and found the place where the prophet Isaiah spoke about God's promise to send a special king who would help the people to live as God intended them to. Jesus read these words.

> *'The Spirit of the Lord is upon me, because he has chosen me to bring good news to the poor. He has sent me to proclaim liberty to the captives and recovery of sight to the blind; to set free the oppressed and announce that the time has come when the Lord will save his people.'*
>
> Luke 4:18–19

When Jesus had finished reading, he sat down. Everyone was looking at him, waiting to hear what he would say next, but Jesus simply said:

> *'This passage of scripture has come true today.'*
>
> Luke 4:21

I wonder what the people thought. What would Jesus say next?

Jesus went on to explain. At first, people thought how well he spoke. But the more he talked about God being his Father and about a new way to love one another, the more angry they became. They said to each other, 'Isn't he the son of Joseph?'

Many of the people in the synagogue that day had known Jesus since he was a little boy. They'd watched him grow up.

And now here he was, claiming to be the new king—the Messiah that the prophet had written about so long ago.

Jesus explained that God's love was not just for the people of Israel, but for everyone. God wanted them to care for all those who were unwell, lonely, or poor—and especially those who were considered to be unlovable.

At this, the people became very angry and they pushed Jesus out of the synagogue. They wanted to throw Jesus over a cliff at the edge of the town, but Jesus turned and walked away from them.

Already Simeon's words about Jesus were coming true.

The people's anger didn't stop Jesus. He went on from town to town, teaching about his heavenly Father's love, and showing people a new way to live.

In the past, God's people had lived their lives by following a set of laws called the Ten Commandments. God had given the commandments to Moses and the Israelites many years before. God's rules helped people to love and to care for one another, to be fair and honest and to love God.

Sometimes it is difficult to keep to rules, especially if they stop us doing what we want to do. But can you imagine what it would be like if there were no rules? Just think what would happen!

Something to think about

Write a list of what you think are good rules on one of the stone shapes, and a list of rules which you find difficult on the other.

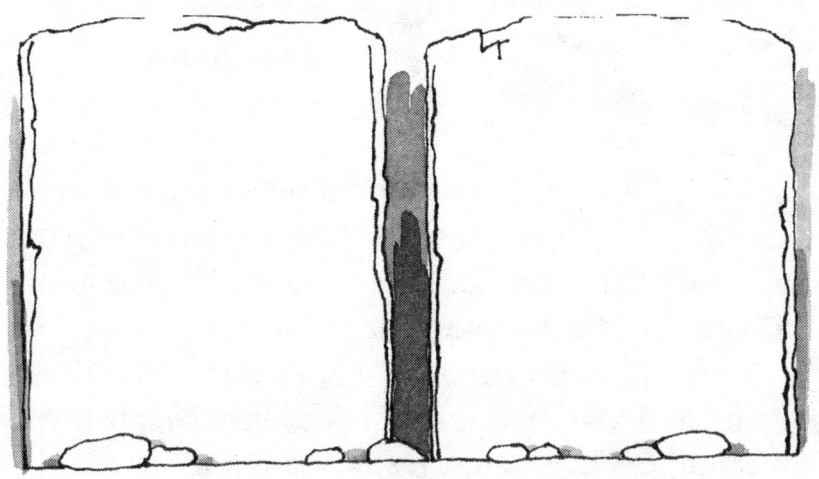

It's often easier to stick to rules when we understand why we are being asked to do so. Then the rules make sense. But Jesus saw that the teachers of the law were making it very difficult for the people to keep to God's rules. The teachers of the law wanted to control people, so they kept on adding more and more rules.

Think what it would be like if you were playing a game and somebody kept changing the rules so that they could win. You would soon get very fed up, wouldn't you? Soon the game would lose all its fun.

That is how it was becoming for the people of Israel. God had given the commandments as a way of helping them to live happily side by side. But somehow God's plan to help people care for one another was being hidden by a long list of dos and don'ts. Soon people were forgetting what was most important.

It was the Sabbath, the day that God had commanded to be a day of rest, a special day to worship God. As usual, Jesus was in the synagogue. Among the crowd that day was a man with a hand that didn't work. Jesus called the man to the front and said to him:

> *'Stretch out your hand.'*
>
> Matthew 12:13

At once, the man stretched out his hand and it was well again, just like his other hand.

Some people in the crowd and the Pharisees, who were the teachers of the law, were very angry when they saw what Jesus had done.

After all, it was the day of rest and it was against the law to do any work! Jesus knew why they were angry, but still he asked them:

> *'What if one of you has a sheep and it falls into a deep hole on the Sabbath? Will you not take hold of it and lift it out? And a human being is worth much more than a sheep!'*
>
> Matthew 12:11–12

Jesus felt sorry for the crowd because he saw that they hadn't really understood how much God loved them. The rules about not working on the day of rest had become more important than caring for people, and that wasn't how God had meant it to be.

Jesus realized he would have to show the people what he meant about caring for one another. The crowds were in for some real surprises!

Love that is full of surprises

Wherever Jesus went, he would be followed by crowds of people. He was different from the other religious teachers. There was something about him that made people want to be with him. It may have been because he told wonderful stories that they walked for miles to listen to him. Or it might have been that he was full of surprises, like the day he turned the water into wine at a friend's wedding. Maybe the crowds followed him because they saw that he was somehow special. He chose ordinary people to be his friends and, most surprising of all, he was able to make those who were unwell healthy again.

As Jesus travelled around, he often came across people who weren't well and people no one cared for. To Jesus, everyone was special. He talked to the people others ignored. He made friends with the people nobody liked. He touched the people nobody wanted. He made people well again.

One day, Jesus was on his way to a town called Jericho. There was a huge crowd with him and along the way he passed a blind man who was sitting by the roadside, begging. The blind man's name was Bartimaeus. When Bartimaeus heard Jesus was coming by, he began to shout out:

> *'Jesus! Son of David! Take pity on me!'*
> Luke 18:38

The crowds were very angry and told Bartimaeus to be quiet. But Jesus stopped and asked them to bring Bartimaeus to him. Imagine the crowd's surprise when they saw Jesus talking to the poor blind man. Jesus asked:

> *'What do you want me to do for you?' 'Sir,' he answered, 'I want to see again.' Jesus said to him, 'Then see! Your faith has made you well.'*
> Luke 18:41–42

At once, Bartimaeus was able to see. He followed Jesus down the road.

Well, what a surprise, not just for Bartimaeus, but also for the crowds who were watching.

Something to think about

How do you think Bartimaeus felt when Jesus told him to see? What do you think the crowd thought about what Jesus had just done?

Fill in the speech bubbles with your answers.

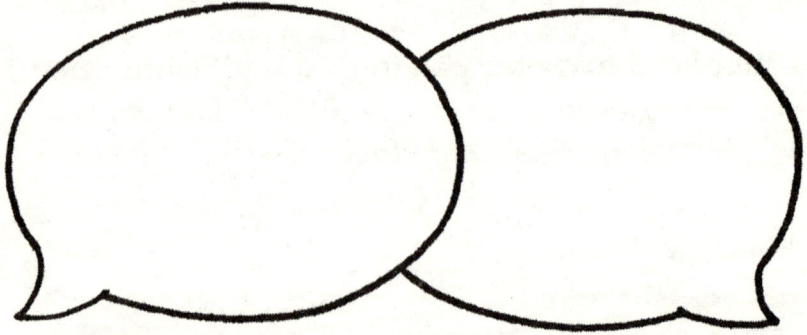

Not everyone was happy about the way Jesus made people well, or about the way he made friends with people who others thought should be ignored.

> *One day when many tax collectors and other outcasts came to listen to Jesus, the Pharisees and the teachers of the Law started grumbling, 'This man welcomes outcasts and even eats with them!'*
>
> Luke 15:1–2

Jesus wanted people to know that God's love and care was for everyone—no matter who they were or what they had done wrong.

So Jesus told them a story about a lost sheep. There were a lot of sheep on the hillsides. Jesus used the story to help people to understand and remember what he was saying.

See if you can help me to tell the story by filling in the missing words.

A shepherd had one hundred 🐑, but one day when he came to count them, he found that there were only ninety-nine. One of the 🐑 was missing. The 👤 thought, I can't leave the missing 🐑 out on the hills all night. A 🦊 might attack it. So the 👤 decided to go and look for the lost 🐑. He looked under 🌳 and behind 🌿, he called and he listened until at last he heard 🐑. The 👤 was so excited at finding the lost 🐑 that he called all his 👥 together for a party.

Jesus told the story to explain to the crowds that everyone was equally important to God. There was nobody that God didn't want to care for.

Let's follow Jesus and see what happened next.

Another day, Jesus was in the temple with his friends. There were many rich men in the temple that day, bringing in their gifts of money to put into the temple moneybox. They seemed to show off as they dropped their money into the box. Suddenly, Jesus noticed a little old lady come shuffling past. Into the moneybox she dropped two tiny copper coins—nothing in comparison to the amount of money the rich men had given. But Jesus said to his friends:

> *'I tell you that this poor widow put in more than all the others. For the others offered their gifts from what they had to spare of their riches; but she, poor as she is, gave all she had to live on.'*
>
> Luke 21:3–4

Jesus wanted the disciples to realize that things aren't always what they seem. The rich men probably wouldn't miss the money they put into the temple moneybox, but the poor old lady showed how much she loved God. She had given him all that she had and kept nothing back for herself.

It's a bit like sharing sweets with a friend. It is easy to share when there are a lot of sweets to go round, but if you only had one sweet left, it might be harder to give it away.

Something to think about

What things could you share with others? Write or draw your answer in the sweets.

Jesus' friends were never quite sure what Jesus would teach them next. He surprised them when he made people better. He surprised them by the things he said. But most of all, he surprised them by turning things upside down.

It was as if things that seemed of little value became special in Jesus' hands—like the widow's coins, and the little lost sheep. People who seemed unimportant to everyone else were very important to Jesus.

They were hard lessons for Jesus' friends to understand, and somehow they kept getting it wrong, like in our next story.

It had been a particularly long and hot day for Jesus, and the crowds were still all around him. Among the crowds were some mothers who had brought their children along, wanting Jesus to touch them and to bless them. When Jesus' friends saw the mothers, they told them to go away, but Jesus heard what was going on and he was very angry.

> *'Let the children come to me, and do not stop them, because the Kingdom of God belongs to such as these.' Then he took the children in his arms, placed his hands on each of them, and blessed them.*
>
> Mark 10:14 and 16

What a surprise for the crowds! The mothers must have been very happy when Jesus called them forward and blessed their children. For Jesus' friends, it was another very important lesson they had to learn. Here was Jesus not only making time for the children, but telling everyone how special and important children are to God and how much God loves them.

No wonder people followed Jesus and wanted to hear what he had to say. His picture of God was so different from anything they had ever heard before. Jesus talked about God being like a father—the very best kind of father you could imagine, someone who was fair, kind and loving to all his children.

The religious teachers of the law at that time had strict rules about the sort of people who should be avoided. Often these were the very people whom Jesus spent the most time with. These were the people, Jesus said, whom God wants us to love.

Many of the people who followed Jesus began to believe in Jesus and what he told them about how much God his Father loved them. But others grew more and more angry and resentful. Jesus upset their comfortable lives. They began to plot against him and tried to find a way to have him killed.

But killing Jesus was only going to show just how very much God loves us. This was going to be the biggest surprise of all.

The battle between love and hate

At a carnival, people dress up and ride through the town on decorated lorries and tractors. The bands march along and everyone lines the street, cheering and waving. Sometimes they wave little flags or throw streamers. You might even have been part of a parade and ridden on one of the floats. It can be very exciting and pretty noisy, a bit like a huge party.

Decorate this picture of a lorry ready to join in the parade.

One day, Jesus was heading for Jerusalem with his friends. He sent two of them into a nearby village with instructions to find a colt (a young donkey) tied up there. When his friends brought the donkey back to Jesus, they threw their coats over the donkey's back and Jesus climbed on.

As Jesus rode on the donkey, everyone suddenly started to wave and cheer. They threw their cloaks on the ground and pulled branches off the palm trees to wave. They shouted, 'Praise God', 'God bless the king who comes in the name of the Lord' and 'Hosanna'. It was just like a carnival, except that instead of brightly coloured floats and bands, there was just Jesus riding on a young donkey.

The people were so pleased to see Jesus. They danced and shouted along the road in front and behind him.

Some of the Pharisees, the teachers of the law, were very angry. They told Jesus to tell the crowds to be quiet.

Jesus often talked using riddles and pictures, and now he said to the Pharisees:

> *'I tell you that if they keep quiet, the stones themselves will start shouting.'*
>
> Luke 19:40

What a funny thing for Jesus to say! What do you think he meant?

Something to think about

Find a nice flat pebble and some brightly coloured paints. On one side of the pebble, paint a smiley face, and on the other side, what you think the stones would have shouted if the crowd had been quiet.

When a great soldier or king came back from battle, he would ride into the village or town on a fine horse, leading his army. The crowds would cheer and celebrate. When Jesus rode into Jerusalem, the crowds cheered and called him their king, but he didn't ride on a horse, just a humble donkey. Another surprise!

Jesus was showing the people that there was another way to live together—not with hatred and fighting, but with love and peace and forgiveness.

But it wasn't long before the anger of those religious leaders towards Jesus began to make the streets of Jerusalem echo with shouts of hate.

The chief priests and teachers of the law were jealous of all the attention Jesus was getting. They tried to find a way to arrest him for saying that he was God's Son. They spread lies about him to the people and soon, instead of cheering Jesus, everyone was shouting, 'Crucify him, crucify him!'

Things were changing. It was going to be a difficult time for Jesus. Remember Simeon's words all those years before when he first held Jesus as a baby? Was this what he had been warning Mary about?

Jesus knew what it felt like when the world was against him. He knew what it was like to be laughed at and spat on, to be beaten and left all alone. But, through it all, Jesus never stopped forgiving those who were hurting him. Even though some of his friends ran away and left him, Jesus never stopped loving them.

One of Jesus' friends was a man called Peter. Peter soon discovered just how very much Jesus loved him.

Something to think about

You could use a small torch to help you in your thinking.

• Jesus came to be like a light in the world, showing us the things that are good and loving. *Switch on the torch*.

But sometimes we are unkind, and that is like shutting out God's love. *Switch off the torch*.

For those times when I am angry… (*switch off the torch*), Lord, help me to remember your love… (*switch on the torch*).

For those times when I ignore those who are hurting… (*switch off the torch*), Lord, help me to remember your love… (*switch on the torch*).

For those times when I make fun of people… (*switch off the torch*), Lord, help me to remember your love… (*switch on the torch*).

For those times when I forget about you… (*switch off the torch*), Lord, help me to remember your love… (*switch on the torch*).

Many years later, Paul wrote in one of his letters:

> *There is nothing in all creation that will ever be able to separate us from the love of God which is ours through Christ Jesus our Lord.*
>
> Romans 8:39

Peter discovers just how much God loves him

This is the story of Peter, one of Jesus' closest friends. As you read his story, try to imagine you are there with him.

Hello! I'm Peter, one of Jesus' disciples. A disciple is someone who follows the teaching of another person. And that is what I did. I knew right from the beginning that there was something special about Jesus. I first met him when I was finishing a day's fishing with my brother, Andrew. We got chatting and the things Jesus said made us decide to go with him. It was too good an opportunity to miss.

You should have seen some of the amazing things Jesus did—like healing people who were ill! He spent time with people who nobody else had time for, and he told the most amazing stories. He told us about God and how much he loved us, and he talked about God being his Father. At first I wasn't sure about that, but gradually I began to realize that Jesus really was God's Son.

One day, Jesus asked us straight out, 'Who do you say I am?' I said, 'You are the Messiah, the Son of the living God.' Well, it seemed obvious to me. Jesus said, 'Good for you, Simon son of John!' Then he started to call me Peter. He said, 'Peter, you are a rock, and on this rock foundation I will build my church, and not even death will ever be able to overcome it. I will give you the keys of the kingdom of heaven.'

Well, I can tell you, now I was really confused! What was all this talk about death? When I look back, I can see that Jesus talked a lot after that about the way he would die. But I don't think any of us really understood what he was saying.

Then there was that awful night when we shared the Passover meal together. This was a special meal to help us remember how God had rescued his people from Egypt, long ago. That night, Jesus seemed different somehow.

As we ate together, he talked about being betrayed, about going away. He said, 'I give you a new commandment: love one another. As I have loved you, so you must love one another.'

I couldn't bear the thought of him going away and told him I was even ready to die for him. Then he said, 'Are you really ready to die for me? Before the cock crows, you will say three times that you do not know me.' Of course, I didn't believe him. How could I do such a thing?

After supper, we went for a walk in the garden close by. We often went there with Jesus. It was such a peaceful place. There was no doubt that Jesus seemed upset that night. He told us to pray with him, but after such a good supper… well, it was hard to keep my eyes open.

Suddenly the quietness of the garden was broken by the sound of angry voices. It was a group of Roman soldiers, carrying flaming torches.

They were armed, and it turned out they had come to arrest Jesus. They looked as if they were expecting a struggle, but Jesus kept very calm. I was scared and angry. I pulled out my sword and struck one of the guards, but Jesus told me to put my sword away. It was a wonder I wasn't arrested too, but they only seemed interested in Jesus. It was awful. They tied him up and led him away like a criminal.

Some of us followed as they took Jesus to the house of the high priest. I got as far as the gate but had to wait there until I got permission to go into the courtyard. There was a girl at the gate and she surprised me by saying, 'Aren't you also one of the disciples of that man?' 'No, I am not,' I said, and went in to warm myself by the fire.

It was a really cold evening. While I stood by the fire, one of the guards asked me again, 'Aren't you also one of the disciples of that man?' I was scared, I can tell you! Again I said, 'No, I am not.' One of the others said, 'Didn't I see you with him in the garden?' Again I said, 'No, I don't know this man.' Just then, a cock crowed in the courtyard and I felt a chill run down my spine.

What had Jesus said while we were having supper...?

I felt so ashamed. I ran from the courtyard, almost blinded by my tears.

The next time I saw Jesus, I could barely recognize him. The streets were full of people, some jeering at him, others crying and wailing. Jesus was being forced to carry a huge wooden cross through the crowd. His body was bruised and bleeding from being beaten and on his head was a crown made from vicious thorns. The soldiers were leading him to a place just outside the city, where he was to be crucified.

I felt so awful. Where had it all gone wrong? How could I have let him down so badly?

After Jesus died on the cross, it seemed as if that was the end. It was all over. Then, three days later, something really surprising happened. Jesus came alive again! I know it's hard to believe—I found it hard to believe, too. But I saw him with my own eyes. When I heard the news, I ran to the tomb where his body had been laid. The tomb was empty!

I'll never forget that morning when I saw Jesus after he had risen from the dead. We'd been out fishing, and as we got near to the land we saw someone standing on the beach. I recognized that it was Jesus standing there. I was so anxious to see him that I leapt out of the boat and waded ashore. Jesus had prepared a fire on the beach and told us to bring some fish so that we could have breakfast together.

After we'd eaten, Jesus said to me, 'Simon, son of John, do you love me more than these others do?' What a question to ask me! But I'd let him down so badly. Perhaps he needed to know.

'Yes, Lord,' I replied. 'You know that I love you.'

Then a second time he asked, 'Simon, son of John, do you love me?'

'Yes, Lord,' I answered again. 'You know that I love you.'

When Jesus asked a third time, 'Simon, son of John, do you love me?' I remembered that awful night when I'd so let Jesus down by saying I didn't know him. I remembered how, even at supper, Jesus had told me that I would let him down three times before the cock crowed.

Then I realized that Jesus was showing me he still loved me and trusted me, even though I'd let him down. Now I said to him, 'Lord, you know everything; you know that I love you!'

Jesus said to me, 'Follow me!'

I determined at that time never to let Jesus down again. I would follow him and I would tell others about him. He was the Son of God! He had shown me just how much God loves me!

Peter discovered that even though he'd let Jesus down, still Jesus' love was big enough to forgive him and to go on loving him.

Today, Jesus still says to us, 'Do you love me? Then listen to me and follow what I ask you to do!'

Jesus loves us so much that he was prepared to die for us. He stretched out his arms wide on the cross. It was as if he was saying, 'This is how much I love you.'

This special kind of love has a Greek name. It is called 'Agape'.

You say it like this: A - ga - pay

A love that never lets go

> *Jesus led his friends out of Jerusalem as far as Bethany, where he raised his hands and blessed them. As he was blessing them, he departed from them and was taken up into heaven.*
>
> Luke 24:50–51

What a mixture of feelings those early disciples must have gone through. First, the horror of seeing Jesus die on the cross. All they'd hoped for must have died too on that awful day. Then, three days later, Jesus is back among them—he has risen from the dead! They can see him, touch him, eat with him and laugh with him.

Jesus must have really encouraged his disciples over those next forty days, for on the day when he finally left them to return to his heavenly Father we find the disciples not hidden away, sad and afraid, but in the Temple, happy and thankful.

> *They worshipped him and went back into Jerusalem, filled with great joy, and spent all their time in the Temple giving thanks to God.*
>
> Luke 24:52–53

I wonder what had changed them. What had Jesus said to them to stop them feeling sad? Does the Bible verse below give us a clue?

> *And when they came together, he gave them this order: 'Do not leave Jerusalem, but wait for the gift my Father promised.'*
>
> Acts 1:4

I like receiving presents, don't you? I like to take time opening the gift and trying to guess what it can be.

We receive gifts at Christmas and birthdays, but those don't have to be the only times. We can give gifts to people to say all kinds of things. See if you can write a different message in each gift tag—the first one is done for you.

The gift that Jesus promised to the disciples wasn't something that could be wrapped up with a gift tag on it. It wasn't a gift that you could hold, but it was a very special kind of gift.

When Jesus had shared that last supper with his disciples, he had told them that he had to leave them to go back to his Father God in heaven. He said that he wasn't going to leave them on their own. He would give them a special gift called the Holy Spirit. The Holy Spirit would live inside each one of them and always be with them. Jesus explained:

> *'The Helper, the Holy Spirit, whom the Father will send in my name, will teach you everything and make you remember all that I have told you.'*
>
> John 14:26

Jesus was trying to explain that even though he couldn't be with them any more, they would never need to feel afraid or alone because the Holy Spirit would be a constant reminder of how much God loved them.

Sometimes we have to wait, knowing that a gift is going to arrive but not knowing what it is or how it will come to us. How does that feel?

Imagine the excitement the disciples must have felt, waiting in Jerusalem for Jesus' promised gift.

And what a surprise they got when it did arrive!
This is how Luke describes it:

> *All the believers were gathered together in one place. Suddenly there was a noise from the sky which sounded like a strong wind blowing, and it filled the whole house where they were sitting. Then they saw what looked like tongues of fire which spread out and touched each person there. They were all filled with the Holy Spirit and began to talk in other languages, as the Spirit enabled them to speak.*
>
> Acts 2:1–4

What a surprise gift!!

There was such a loud noise that people outside came to see what was happening. People living in Jerusalem at that time were from all different parts of the world, so imagine their surprise when they heard the disciples talking to them in their own languages!

Fill in the surprised expressions on the disciples' faces as they received the gift of the Holy Spirit.

Two thousand years later, we still celebrate that special day when the disciples received the gift of the Holy Spirit. It is called Pentecost, and we sometimes think of it as the Church's birthday.

It was on the day of Pentecost that the disciples began to do what Jesus had told them to do:

> 'Go, then, to all peoples everywhere and make them my disciples.'
>
> Matthew 28:19

The Bible tells us that when Peter talked to the crowds that day about Jesus, some three thousand people decided to become followers of Jesus.

From then on, the story of Jesus began to spread, not just through Jerusalem, but into other countries as well.

Do you remember the day Jesus was thrown out of the synagogue for saying that God's love was for all people everywhere, not just the Israelites? Now his words were coming true. The message that Jesus gave of God's love was beginning to spread all around the world.

Two thousand years later, the story of Jesus has been passed on from one person to another. The story has spread from that little town of Bethlehem where Jesus' story began, throughout the whole world.

Over the centuries, churches have been built where, Sunday by Sunday, Christians come together to learn more about the stories of Jesus and to find out how much God loves us.

Look in the flames of fire to see some of the different ways the Holy Spirit still helps us today.

To help us to know that God loves us

To help us to care for other people

To help us to know the difference between right and wrong

To help us to tell others about Jesus

Do you remember how the disciples discovered that Jesus was able to change the smallest thing into something special? Jesus said two little words to his disciples.

'Follow me!'

I wonder if the disciples realized just how far God's message of love would spread? With the help of God's special gift, the Holy Spirit, it is still being passed on, two thousand years later!

Today, Jesus is saying those same two little words to us.

'Follow me!'

Now, with the help of the Holy Spirit, we too can be part of the sharing of God's everlasting story—a story that tells how much God loves everyone, whoever they are.

And that's not all. If you listen deep inside yourself, you'll be surprised to hear the Holy Spirit whisper:

'God's love is full of surprises!'